EMPTY NESTER...

I THINK NOT!

Experiencing Joy in this Fresh Season of Life

D1522542

Written by Dr. Abby Volmer

TABLE OF CONTENTS

PROLOGUE

When my youngest son (I have three) was making plans to go to college, he decided on a university that was only about 30 minutes from our house. His two other brothers had moved to schools about two hours away. "That's awesome!" I told him. "I can come and watch you play intramural games!!" His response?

"Uhh, no you can't, Mom."

"What do you MEAN?"

"I mean, nope."

Wait a minute! Going to my kids' activities had filled my life for the past twenty-two years! I was a booster mom. I attended all concerts or shows. All the teachers and coaches knew me and enlisted my help when needed. I was a PART of my kids' lives! I cheered them on and gave them all the support a mother is supposed to give. Now the only one I still had at home, the only one "left," my baby... just told me to back off. Huh. Okay. I can take a hint. *gut punch *buzzing in the head pursues.

Empty Nest Syndrome is a real thing. As the Mayo Clinic describes it, Empty Nest Syndrome is not a clinical diagnosis as much as a phenomenon experienced by a parent's sense of loss and sadness when their last child leaves home (MFMER, 2020). Empty Nest Syndrome symptoms can include feeling a loss of purpose and sadness, even depression. A parent might feel frustration at now finding loss of control (read "helicopter parent just lost his or her landing zone"), Commonly, a parent might feel worried and intense anxiety over a child's well-being without them there. I mean, we went to college, right? We KNOW! The last child leaving can be a parent's nightmare...if you let it.

But there are things we can do and attitudes we can adopt that can bring us into a new and positive realm of life. A realm where we can enjoy our marriage, our own time, and still enjoy our children. We can. I promise. The intent of this book is to lead you there.

CHAPTER I

Pivot Your Focus: Reconnecting with Your Partner

"A successful marriage requires falling in love many times, always with the same person."

– Mignon McLaughlin

I am embarrassed to admit this, but while we were raising our children, I almost lost my husband along the way. I poured my energy into my children, my work, my church, my extended family, and then...my husband. In that order. That's messed up, but it is honest. So when that last kid packed up his car and was pulling away, my mind said, "Are you kidding me? Just me and him? From now on? Every day? Forever?" But something special actually came from that separation from daily life with kids.

There is another known phenomenon inside Empty Nest called Empty Nest Divorce (Griefandsympathy.com, 2012-2020). Parents find themselves together, alone, for the first time in years. Maybe they don't have as much in common as they used to. Maybe they have developed separate hobbies and lifestyles the other is not involved in. Perhaps hormones are changing, and negative feelings are strong. I had to cipher this out for my own marriage. I mean, I had made a vow in the presence of God to stay with this man until death do us part. Was divorce where my husband and I were headed? Because we certainly weren't connected.

I sat down and asked myself some important questions. Number One: Did I care about my husband? Answer: Of course. Number Two: Did I love him? Yes, I did. Number

Three: Was that love manifested in how we interacted with each other? No, it wasn't. Number Four: Would I prefer to go home alone or have him there to go home to? Answer...and this is a big one...I would prefer to have him to come home to rather than to be alone. And finally, "What could I personally change to fix our relationship? Not, what could HE change (and trust me, I had a laundry list of those items in my head), but rather what could I do. The answer to that final question brought about amazing, unforeseen consequences.

SUGGESTION ONE: Intentional Focus and Active Listening

After much thought and prayer (I am a praying woman, even if I have the mouth of a sailor), I decided that I needed to FOCUS on my husband. Not necessarily by DOING things for him, but really focus on what he had to say. I decided I had just spent twenty years listening and looking at him from the corner of my eye, which was usually fixed on someone (or something) else. He had been in my peripherals. I was going to look at him while he talked to me. I was going to look him in the eye when he talked about work and actively listen to what he was saying. I was going to respond with support, not suggestions, with affirmation, not condemnation. This was it. This was where I was going to begin to reconnect with my husband.

The response was mind-blowing. As I began to really listen to my husband and positively respond to his conversations, to affirm and support him, the same thing came back to me trifold. It was like a switch was flipped. The connection that had been missing in my marriage, which I then GAVE, was reciprocated. It was like he had just been waiting for me to see him again. It was exciting but sad. I realized that all these years when I had blamed him for so much negativity could perhaps have manifested from me. I had ignored his need to be seen and heard, and he had responded with sharpness and bitterness. This listening, this "seeing" was healing.

So, while it might sound "therapy-ish" (I'm sure that's a word), I highly recommend you give intentional focus and active listening to your partner a try. It is probably something you will need to practice and often revisit. I find myself having to consciously return to it even now. But from my personal experience, it is so worth it. It was life-changing for my husband and me.

SUGGESTION TWO: The Real Meat is in the Everyday. Live it.

I've read many articles for empty-nesters telling them to travel, see the world, do the things they always dreamed of. And I one hundred percent agree with that! But...the real meat, the real happiness, the real joy in life is found in the everyday. To reconnect with your partner, you need to reconnect on a daily level. Don't wait for the big things to happen. Make the little things big.

For example, cook meals together and play the kinds of music you both grew up with while doing so. Sing lines together. Laugh. Tease. Steal a quick kiss. Give a loving pat. Don't wait for your partner to do these things for you. Don't even expect them. Just give them. And give them. And give them. Oh, the places you will go.

Sit outside together. If he or she likes to work outside or in the garage, pull up a chair for a bit. Talk about the yard and the house and memories. Giggle at the pets. This, my friends, is where you find happiness in post-children marriage. We live in the country and have a long driveway. Some of my favorite memories are my husband listening to a baseball game on the radio while I ride my bike in circles in the drive, or walk on my stilts, or jump on my pogo stick. Granted, not the most mature sorts of activities, but we were doing together what we like to do separately. And we reconnected.

SUGGESTION THREE: Learn About Something Your Partner Enjoys

By this time in life, there have got to be subjects your partner knows a lot about that you know little. Learn about them. Enough to hold a simple conversation. Let him or her teach you a bit. That doesn't mean badger him or her with questions while a game is playing. But maybe do something like learn the names of a few key players and their positions. Or if your partner likes to grill, learn about some different techniques. If yard work is something they do on the weekend, ask about the supplies they use.

Now, I am not suggesting that you barge into their personal space and demand a spot there. Absolutely not. Everyone needs their space and their thing. I am suggesting, however, that you learn enough about whatever that thing might be to carry on a decent conversation. That's all. If that was your child involved in an activity, would you have learned about it? I know I did. I came away from my children's "at-home" years knowing so much more about football than I had ever known before. I learned about it because it was important to my kids, and I was interested in them. The same can hold true for your partner.

SUGGESTION FOUR: Give in Now and Then

There it is. There's not much more I can add to that. It is a simple concept but a difficult action. Give in once in a while. It doesn't have to be always. In fact, it shouldn't be always. But occasionally, give in. Say, okay, we will do it your way. This can be as simple as the way to cut the onions, the parking spot to choose from, or the way to fold the towels. Just give in once in a while. It makes for a partnership.

And along those same lines, learn to say "I'm sorry." Not "I'm sorry, but.." Just, "I'm sorry." Set an example of what mature interactions are made of. Hopefully, that will be reciprocated. My husband really taught me this at the beginning of our marriage. I was one of those strong-willed 30-somethings who, deep down, felt that if I apologized, it was admitting I was wrong...and I wasn't...ever. But truth be told, sometimes I was wrong. And sometimes I wasn't, but my actions were wrong. Or sometimes I was right, my actions were right, but I was sorry the whole thing even happened. My husband taught me to say I'm sorry by example. And when he apologized, I usually responded back with an apology as well. And I found that when I apologized, he usually did too.

It takes changes in your behavior to reconnect with your spouse. That's all you really have control of. These suggestions do not make a person lose themselves or their own identity. Not if they are done with love and in balance. They, instead, build a relationship.

CHAPTER SUMMARY:

1. SUGGESTION ONE: Give your partner your intentional focus and actively listen

2. SUGGESTION TWO: The Real Meat is in the Everyday. Do the everyday things that rebuild a marriage

3. SUGGESTION THREE: Learn About Something Your Partner Enjoys

4. SUGGESTION FOUR: Give in Now and Then

CHAPTER II

Finding Your Own Space Without Pushing Others Out

"It's never too late to be what you might have been."

~George Elliot

Notice I put this chapter AFTER reconnecting with your partner. Trouble often brews when we search for and find our own space, but inadvertently push away our partner. Make both reconnecting with your partner and finding your own space priorities. They are both important in this fresh season of life. Just don't do one at the expense of the other.

SUGGESTION ONE: Modulate Your Priorities

So, I am not going to tell you to "prioritize" what is important because that suggests a hierarchy, and I don't think it is a proper way of viewing what is important in life. Instead, I like to think of prioritizing more in terms of modulating the important things, with one exception. Let's take a look at what I mean.

For me, there are four important things in my life: My faith, my family, my work, and my activities. Some might say to prioritize those, but I simply cannot prioritize them as a one-time overall list...with one exception: My faith. I truly believe and have experienced that before anything in my life can be filled with peace and joy, God needs to be present. So, I prioritize my time in scripture and prayer and church to stay close to God, BUT then God is interwoven in all the other important parts of my life. He doesn't just sit at the apex of a priority triangle as a lone component.

He weaves in and out of everything important in my life as it comes.

So, while I do believe that if peace is to come to my life, God must be present, I also don't believe my time in scripture and prayer, and the church compartmentalizes him. I want to recognize him in all parts of my life. Then, and here is where I differ from others, I believe we should modulate the other components of our life in importance or priority depending upon the situation. Let me give some examples.

Let's say you get a call in the middle of the night from the police department at your child's university town. At that moment, your child becomes the priority in your life. Giving your husband a full night's sleep is not priority. Your work tomorrow is not priority. Right now, helping your child reigns supreme in your life. Where is God in that? He is there. Right smack in the middle. He is there as you dress. He is there as you drive. He is there as your comfort. He is not sitting in a book or waiting for morning prayer. He is right there in the moment. So, in this example, your children (or child in this case) is your priority, and God is present.

Let's give another example. Let's say one of my kids comes home from school for the summer and him and his dad get into a disagreement over putting tools away. My husband becomes my priority. I am not going to undercut him in front of the children. I am going to support him in his needs. We might talk later alone. We might develop plans and talk to our son together later, but at that moment, my husband is my priority...and God is there. He is there in the interactions...in our responses...in our anger...in our peace. In this example, my husband is my priority, but God is present.

A working example might be as follows. Let's say I have a presentation the next day and something is wrong with my technology. I turn to my family and tell them I will not be making dinner, I will not be proofreading papers, and I will not be going to my art lesson that evening. At this point in time, my work is my priority until my presentation is fixed. Is God there? Oh boy, I hope so. We pray him into everything we do.

A final example might be my activities. It is my routine to get my exercise done in the morning. In that way, I don't skip it, and it starts my day off right. If kids are home from school, they may have to wait a while if they want breakfast, or they can fix their own. My husband might talk to me about his work after my workout. Right now, at that moment, my priority is self-care. Is God with me? Always. Is that selfish? No! Not unless I put that before something that *is* more important at the moment. For instance, if my son is going for a job interview and his car won't start, am I going to make him wait for my help until I'm done working out? Of course not. Another example might be, am I going to prioritize working out over going to church on Sunday? Nope. We need to modulate our priorities based upon the circumstances.

So, as you see, although I say to make God the number one priority, what I really mean is to make prayer, church, and scripture reading a priority, and then allow the Holy Spirit to weave Himself into everything else in your life. Then modulate the other important things in your life based on circumstances: modulate their priority...but keep God present always.

SUGGESTION TWO: Review Your Dreams of Yesteryears

After my youngest left for school, I took a survey of my dreams of yesteryears. What did young Abby dream of for her future? What had she achieved and what could still be done? At that point, I decided to return to university and get my Doctorate degree. I was from a family of scholars, and having a Doctorate was something I had always hoped for myself. But doing so is a big undertaking as well as a time sucker. I had never felt able to give that time before. So I applied to the University of Missouri and was accepted into their program. There are other learning options available now that don't require such a commitment. All the Masterclass courses available online sound so interesting and are taught by famous experts in their fields. They run from two to four hours each and are under $200 per course. The range of topics is amazing! I would suggest doing a little online research to find ones that others recommend before spending your money.

A positive about being in this season of life is time. You now have the time to devote to something other than your kids. What could you do with that time? When you were young and hopeful, where did you see yourself at this age? Is it still attainable? Look at the financial requirements. Weigh the time commitments. If it is important to you, make a plan.

SUGGESTION THREE: Take Control of Your Health and Wellness

Another thing that happened in my early empty-nester years was in the area of health and wellness. I will speak more about this in Chapter 4. Throughout the years of parenting, I had gained a huge amount of weight: 100 lbs. actually. So at the age of 52, I decided enough was enough. I had to make a change if I wanted to get down on the floor with future grandchildren, or if I didn't want to be a burden to my family in old age. I had a few health scares, and I was ready to make that change. So I hired a personal trainer and, through diet and exercise, lost 100 pounds. If you are interested in how I did it, you can pick up my book from Amazon *How to Lose 100 Pounds After the Age of 50: By someone who actually did.*

The weight loss and health commitment were something I still cherish today. It has changed my life. I have been able to go on the sorts of vacations with my family that I would never have been able to do before. I have hiked and rafted and explored and climbed and ziplined. I have run races and obstacle courses. I have competed in Power Lifting. I feel capable of taking on new challenges that present themselves. It is not only that the weight is gone. It is that the weight loss has given me a life in my 50's that I wouldn't have been able to have before. Most importantly, one that I can share with my family.

You might wonder how to get started. Find someone who has been successful and ask them what they did. Who did they have to support them? Maybe there is a nutritionist or trainer they used who they would recommend.

Begin with walking. It is something that everyone can do and is so good for you. Build your distance and level of intensity through time. Listen to beautiful music as you walk or inspiring podcasts. There is such an abundance of great apps you can use to listen while you walk. Find a pretty trail of you can. If you enjoy walking with others, find a buddy to walk with you, but that isn't necessary.

Then begin to monitor the types of food you are eating. Prioritize lean protein since that helps you feel full. Have eggs o egg whites for breakfast. Maybe buy a protein powder for shakes at mid-morning. Eat lean meat, fruit, a vegetable, some nuts, and maybe a yogurt for lunch. Drink a protein shake and eat a piece of fruit mid-afternoon. Then eat a healthy dinner at night that includes a vegetable. Sip a caffeine-free tea later in the evening.

This is how you can get started. You don't have to make huge changes all at one time. Just decide to eat like a healthy person. Not a skinny person, but a healthy person.

Take control of your health and wellness. We are all at different levels and our experiences will all be different.

But if I could give you one suggestion, it would be to take control of your health. Your future depends on it.

SUGGESTION FOUR: Find Peace Outside Yourself - Volunteer and Pray

I am a Christian, and from that faith comes the calling to help others. After the children leave is the perfect time to become more heavily involved in your church or social justice programs. I'm not suggesting that the time before that is not, but I AM saying from experience that I have more time now to dedicate than I might have in my past years. Church and volunteer work is an amazing place to focus attention. As long as you keep your focus on giving and not on controlling, the rewards are immense.

Someone might think, "Oh, I caught that, Abby. What did you mean by 'controlling?'" Well, sadly through the years I have seen amazing people begin great work only to want things all done their way to the detriment of the culture and climate of the program. I mention this at the risk of veering from the subject of this book. But I mention it as a warning. Take heed. Be careful. Bring glory, not drama.

Finally, find time to sit alone with God, be that through prayer, scripture or faith reading, song, or any combination of the above. If we can center ourselves on what is important OUTSIDE of ourselves, we can find peace. We were created not to find peace through ourselves, but to find it in God. Take time to find it.

SUGGESTION FIVE: Begin a New or Revive a Lost Hobby

This one sounds like a cliche, but seriously, keep your eyes open for interests. Maybe you have an old talent you would like to revive. Or maybe you have a sport you would like to take up. Or perhaps you love antiquing and want to open a booth or repurpose for Etsy. Keep your eyes open for opportunities and try what sounds interesting. You don't have to commit to it. The fun is in the trying. And you might make new friends as well!

I have two friends who grew up with an auctioneer father. Now they attend auctions and repurpose items for antique stores. I have another friend who is an outdoor enthusiast. She swims, bikes, runs, or kayaks regularly. I always wanted to write. Look at me. Self-publishing has given me the opportunity to write and revise two books.

Join a club! I am a member of a book club that meets nine times a year. It is something I look forward to with great enthusiasm.

Truly, this time of your life can be a blessing. Embrace it as such. Experience what you have never given yourself time to have. Play. Connect. Pray. Grow.

CHAPTER SUMMARY:

1. SUGGESTION ONE: Modulate Your Priorities

2. SUGGESTION TWO: Review Your Dreams of Yesteryear

3. SUGGESTION THREE: Take Control of Your Health and Wellness

4. SUGGESTION FOUR: Volunteer and Pray

5. SUGGESTION FIVE: Find a Hobby

CHAPTER III

Maintain What is Under the Hood - Body Maintenance

"To keep the body in good health is a duty…otherwise we shall not be able to keep the mind strong and clear."

– Buddha

If I want my car to have a longer life, I provide regular and consistent maintenance. That means I change the oil and filters regularly. I use quality gasoline. And I get things fixed when the red light comes on. If I want a high resale value, I take care of the exterior and interior, but those won't give my car longevity. What will is taking care of what makes it run.

With this stage of our life come some physical changes that aren't, shall I say, welcomed. It is a fact that the body ages, and with that aging come physical changes. For example, our lean body mass decreases and as we head into menopause, our fat distribution tends to accumulate around the mid-section. Our metabolism in general begins to slow down as well. Arthritis occurs in 23% of adults. That is 54 million people (CDC. 2020). These are physical changes that occur with aging. We should not grieve them, but begin to understand them.

What scientists are not completely sure of, however, is the cause of some changes. Are these changes inevitable, or can we do something about some of them? For example, is our metabolism slowing because we are getting older, or is it because our lifestyle includes less movement and more sitting? Is our lean body mass going to shrivel away, or can we restore some of it with strength or resistance training? The research is finding that a change in our lifestyle can have a huge effect on these processes.

SUGGESTION ONE: Get Moving

If I am completely honest with myself, I have to say that I am very comfortable being comfortable. I LIKE sitting in my recliner with a bowl of ice cream (chocolate chips included) binge-watching Parenthood. I enjoy relaxing on the deck with a book and a glass of wine. However, if I do not counteract these sedentary activities with some movement, my body is going to adapt negatively. My metabolism will slow. My muscles will atrophy. My joints will tighten. And if I do this for years, my body's aging process will quicken.

But the good news is that you don't have to completely give up these times of relaxation. Just some of it. Walk, or run, or bicycle. You need to move your joints and muscles.

You need to do some type of resistance exercises, be that bodyweight programs, resistance bands, dumbbells, or even Cross Fit. When you empty the dishwasher, do five squats. When you pull out the laundry, take a minute to stretch your hamstrings. When you pass a door jamb, grab hold and gently stretch your shoulders and chest. You need to stretch and flex. These are natural movements that keep you "oiled" so to speak.

SUGGESTION TWO: Try To Maintain a Healthy Weight

I don't believe there is a contemporary adult out there who hasn't heard the links of obesity to health issues. The World Health Organization delineates the possible consequences clearly: heart disease, stroke, diabetes, and osteoarthritis. This is not where we hope to head in our fresh season of life.

But even though we get this, maintaining a healthy weight is so much more than just the math of calories in and calories out. There are emotions and environmental issues. There are stressors and genetics. There are habits and lifestyles. All of these play a human role in maintaining a healthy weight. However, a simple place to begin is to try and find how many calories you burn a day and how many you consume. From there you can begin to make small changes with big impacts.

To find how many calories you burn, many health apps ask you to categorize your activity level. Is it highly Active, moderately active, lightly active, or sedentary? This is often based on how active your job is and how often you move. But it can be difficult to quantify in regards to how many calories your intake (your diet) and how many your burn (metabolism). Smartwatches and fitness trackers can more accurately do the data crunching for you. I use a Fit Bit, but most of my friends and family use an Apple Watch.

Both are superb and monitoring and averaging your calories burned.

So what I have done is to use my Fit Bit to determine my daily calories burned and then I use the app My Fitness Pal to log my calorie intake. From that comparison, I have determined an approximate caloric intake I need to maintain or lose weight. Is it the perfect formula? No, but it sure is helpful. I have found my intake to burn ratio has changed from when I was younger. I have had to adjust.

As I have grown older, my metabolism (how many calories I burn) has dropped. Again, is the cause aging or lifestyle? I'm not sure. What I AM sure of is that I can't stop aging, but I CAN change my lifestyle

SUGGESTION THREE: Eat Anti-Inflammatory Foods

Additionally, the body can begin to turn on itself with inflammation. As I mentioned earlier, 54 million people are reported to have Arthritis. More than 24 million are limited in their activities, and more than 1 in 4 people with Arthritis report joint pain (CDC, 2020). Those are some tough numbers, however, there are things we can do to alleviate the inflammation including diet.

Foods high in sugar content aggravate inflammation. Anti-inflammatory foods, however, decrease it. These foods include fish, nuts and seeds, fruits and vegetables, olive oil, beans, whole grains (Arthritis Foundation).

SUGGESTION FOUR: Follow the Lead of Pro-Aging Women

I follow several pro-aging accounts on Instagram. They are positively inspiring. One entitled *"Women of the New Generation"* highlights active women of the older generation who are still killing it with their activities and achievements! It is so inspiring. Then there are others like *"And Bloom, Aging in Style, An Intentional Age, Healthy*

Happy 50, The Pro Age Woman" and so many more. All of these accounts highlight the positive parts of aging. They are not anti-aging accounts, but rather pro-aging. They show that as women grow older, particularly after menopause, there is still so much we can achieve.

SUGGESTION FIVE: Hydrate

Can someone tell me why I find this one so hard? It really is a simple task and the benefits (amongst others) are lubricating joints, regulating temperature, higher energy levels, and brain function, and pumping blood to muscles. This is something all of us should do. It's best to sip your water throughout the day. This promotes absorption and less restroom time.

In summary, you might be wondering why I have included an entire chapter of an empty-nester book on health and wellness. It is because, at this point in our lives, health and wellness are part of what will bring us joy. We will be able to do the fun things we now have time to do when we can move our bodies properly. Additionally, we are setting a baseline of health for our future. You do not have to be an athlete from your younger years. You can take control now to be the best you can be.

CHAPTER SUMMARY

1. SUGGESTION ONE: Get Moving

2. SUGGESTION TWO: Try to maintain a healthy weight

3. SUGGESTION THREE: Eat Anti-Inflammatory Foods

4. SUGGESTION FOUR: Follow the Lead of Pro-Aging Women

5. SUGGESTION FIVE: Hydrate

CHAPTER IV

Transition Your Role as a Parent

"I admit I've always had trouble taking responsibility for my actions.
But I blame my parents for that."

~Mike Peters – Mother Goose and Grimm

That's a funny quote. It really doesn't have a lot to do with the theme of this chapter, but it made me laugh. What I really want to talk about is not how we raise our children, but rather how our relationship changes when they become adults. There is a great article from the website theextramile.hartford.com called "Adult Children: The Guide to Parenting Your Grown Kids" from which I will largely draw upon (Hartford, 2021). In fact, I will follow the article's suggestions while adding to the clarifications.

SUGGESTION ONE: Respect your differences

The time has passed for you to try to mold your child into your ways. If he or she has not accepted them previously, it is unlikely they will now. I once heard a friend tell her daughter what was wrong with how she was cutting her watermelon. The daughter said, "But my kids like to eat it off the rind." She replied, "But you will have all those rinds lying around to deal with." Okay, stop. This is the exact kind of irritating "advice" that will make your child not want you around. She is not you. The Western Culture is not a culture that truly celebrates the wisdom of the older generation. Accept your adult child for who they are, celebrate those differences, and love them outwardly and wholly.

SUGGESTION TWO: Share Your Wisdom Gracefully (If you must)

Parenting an adult child is an exercise in verbal restraint. If you must share your wisdom, first make sure it is important. Like my watermelon cutting example, let your adult child do things their way. It may not be the most efficient way, but it is their way. By telling them how YOU do it, they might perceive your advice as criticism. The best path for sharing wisdom is more through modeling. If your adult child sees that you are doing something well, they may emulate it. But if they don't, guess what. That is okay.

Now, if they come to you asking for advice, that also must be handled with grace. It is usually a case when there is a problem. You might open the conversation (that THEY initiated) with what you see them doing well. Then begin with something like, "Well, what worked for me, (I don't know if it would work in your case), but what sometimes worked for me was to…" It is important that they see you as a partner and not as the fount of knowledge. Well, they might never see you as the fount of knowledge. Just be a partner and SHARE versus advise.

SUGGESTION THREE: Set Boundaries with Your Adult Child

Because your child has become your friend does not mean that you should share everything with him or her. For example, you should not discuss your spousal issues with your adult child if that spouse is their other parent. This can often bring disharmony and discomfort to your relationship. Also, if your adult child is speaking to you in a disrespectful manner, let them know that is not how you wish to be spoken to. Ask them to please speak to you as they would another adult in their life. Then model that behavior back to them.

SUGGESTION FOUR: Do Things You Love Together

Two of my sons and I love theater and music. My husband, not so much. So the three of us purchase tickets to area events and spend some evenings together. My daughter-in-law and I, along with my mom, sister, and niece, took a trip to Amish country to purchase from the store and greenhouse. Shop, cook, workout, race, read the same book, go to church, drink wine, go to sporting events...just find things to do together that you both love. Or even better, find NEW hobbies or activities to enjoy together. Remember, the meat is in the "now." This is your life. Enjoy it with your kids.

SUGGESTION FIVE: Make Room for Significant Others in Their Life

I cannot emphasize this enough. Your nuclear family is GOING to be disrupted. Your children are GOING to bring in significant others. That is the way of life. It is your responsibility to create harmony and hospitality. What if you don't like them? Do it anyway! They are your child's choice. Talk to them without grilling them. Laugh with them. Ask for their help. Ask for their advice and then follow it. Meld together traditions. If their family always opens gifts on Christmas Eve and they want to do that with you, do it. I'm not kidding. My daughter-in-law is the gateway to my son and to my grandchildren. I will do nothing to harm my relationship with her. In doing so, I would be harming my relationship with my son who would, if the case ever came to be, choose his wife over me. That is the fact. And truthfully, that is how it should be.

"As is written in Genesis 2:24 "Therefore a man shall leave his father and mother and be joined to his wife, and they shall become one flesh." Do not pit your adult child against his or her spouse. You will lose in the end.

SUGGESTION SIX: Be a Consultant, Not a CEO

This suggestion really harkens back to the others. But let's take a look at how a consultant enters into a company. A consultant NEVER just joins a company without being asked. A consultant is usually solicited when there is an unresolved problem. A consultant begins by first assessing how this company is unique and what is happening in this particular situation. The consultant does not come in with blanket advice. The consultant works from the ground level to elicit buy-in. This is done by allowing the company involvement and shares in ideas. The consultant checks in periodically to see how things are going. The job of the consultant is not to remain in the company forever, but to support the company through fixing its own problems and then pulling out.

I mention these things as not a perfect parallel or metaphor, but rather to emphasize the point that even when you are asked for advice, remember that you are not "fixing" the problem. You are there as a sounding board, as a prompter of questions, and hopefully, as a support from which your adult child can find their own solutions. This brings me to our next suggestion.

SUGGESTION SEVEN: Be a Sounding Board for Your Adult Children

Often our adult kids just need to sound off. They need a person they can talk to about what is frustrating them. When they do this, they are often not seeking advice, only someone to listen to them. But here is the important piece. Keep a poker face. If they are talking negatively about their spouse, do NOT jump in with your own negativity about their spouse. They will remember that when they are no longer upset. Simply restate what they are saying. You can even ask if there is anything they would like you to do to help. But be a non-judgmental ear for them. They need that.

SUGGESTION EIGHT: Try to Be Available for Them as Much as You Can Without Too Much Disruption of Your Life

My kids often need me to babysit. If it is at ALL possible, I say yes. Now, if I have a previous engagement that I cannot change, I will say no. But I will say yes as much as I can. Why? Well, first, I adore being with my grandchildren. But secondly, what if they quit asking? If my phone rings, and it is my adult son, I always answer. Why? What if he quit calling? If my youngest wants me to read over an email he is going to send, you bet I will. Why? What if he asks someone else? I want my children in my life. I want them to know I am available to them. So, even if things come at a somewhat inconvenient time, I make the time. Why? Because I'm their mom...

CHAPTER SUMMARY:

What I have provided is a general, shortlist of parenting adult children. I realize it does not include special concern issues that might arise, such as when a child moves back home or has mental or health issues or is in danger. It provides only an overview of suggestions for typical interactions with adult children.

1. SUGGESTION ONE: Respect your differences

2. SUGGESTION TWO: Share Your Wisdom Gracefully (If you must)

3. SUGGESTION THREE: Set Boundaries with Your Adult Child

4. SUGGESTION FOUR: Do Things You Love Together

5. SUGGESTION FIVE: Make Room for Significant Others in Their Life

6. SUGGESTION SIX: Be a Consultant, not a CEO

7. SUGGESTION SEVEN: Be a Sounding Board for Your Adult Children

8. SUGGESTION EIGHT: Try to Be Available for Them as Much as You Can Without Too Much Disruption of Your Life

CONCLUSION:

So, there you have it. This period of time in your life is not an ending, but rather a transition. And what lies ahead can be exciting and interesting and just as full of all the love you have shared in the previous years. Empty Nest? I Think Not

References:

Center for Disease and Control. *Arthritis.* Retrieved September 2021

https://www.cdc.gov/chronicdisease/resources/publicati ons/factsheets/arthritis.htm#:~:text=In%20the%20United %20States%2C%2023,arthritis%20report%20severe%20jo int%20pain.

Mayo Foundation for Medical Education and Research. (2020, April 14). *Tips for coping*

with empty nest syndrome. Mayo Clinic. Retrieved September 22, 2021

https://www.mayoclinic.org/healthy-lifestyle/adult-health/in-depth/empty-nest-syn

drome/art-20047165.

Paturel, Amy. *The Ultimate Arthritis Diet.* Arthritis Foundation. Retrieved September,

2021.https://www.arthritis.org/health-wellness/healthy-living/nutrition/anti-inflammatory/the-ultimate-arthritis-diet

Postle, E. & Postle, L. *Empty Nest Divorce*. Retrieved September 2021

https://www.griefandsympathy.com/emptynestdivorce.html

Sietzer, Michelle. (2021, September 13). Adult Children: The Guide to Parenting Your

Grown Kids. The Hartford Extra Mile. Retrieved September 2021

https://extramile.thehartford.com/family/parenting/parenting-adult-children/

World Health Organization. (2013, March 14). *Obesity: Health Consequences of Being*

Overweight. Retrieved September, 2021 https://www.who.int/news-room/q-a-detail/obesity-health-consequences-of-being-overweight

Made in the USA
Middletown, DE
26 June 2022